# sometimes

choose the sword Press * copyright 2014
ctspress.com

**C.P.**

sometimes
love is
the poison
pushing
itself through
my veins
& i feel
it slowly

murdering
me.

& i am
okay
with that

\*

sometimes i
pull the pillow
into the lock
box of my chest
- how i held you
often (not enough)
until you dipped
down into dreams
something
about ninjas
& unicorns. i always
wake wishing it
was your cigarettes
biting at my nose
& not just feathers
& yesterdays tears

sometimes i
wonder over
the what ifs
that overflow my
lungs & life - fill
it in smog & smothering
regrets. choking on
possibilities i've aborted
& no one wants
to die wondering

sometimes i
sit on my hand
15 minutes total
& jerk off.  they
call it the stranger
- that's pretty self
explanatory

sometimes i
push my wishes
toward the nights
stars.  that works
- right?  & most
often i can't see
stars & Angelina Jolie
won't take my calls
anymore or
ever

sometimes i
want to give in
to the earths dirt
pull. allowing its arms
to wrap me in it's
special sort of love
- no thanks

sometimes
we exchange glances
with the same
moon

& most nights
i roll your name
off my lips
push it into
a whisper & toss
it into the navy
sky asking
her to deliver my letters
of love into your arms

& most nights
i listen to the wind
waiting to see
when my name is called

& most nights
all i hear in response
is my own thoughts

sometimes love
isn't enough
to delete
the pains

& sometimes love
is that pain

∗

sometimes the love
overfills my heart
and spills out over
through my chocolate
truffle eyes

& you can tell
as they try to massage
the pink of your lips

sometimes your eyes
spill pain
down your blouse

kisses caress
all pain into
the away

& i want
my lips to whisper
"aways" into your heart
forever

or
at the least
until i need
chap stick

sometimes my mouth
shares time with
a bottle & vodka
is how i pour love
into your hearts
glass

so, let's get drunk

*

sometimes
she leaves
pieces of her
stranded in my
shirt or in the
sink or tangled
in my own
hair

& sometimes
i want to collect
these stories
reading them back
to myself at night
before dreams invade
my sealed eyes
but. that's
kinda weird
so i bind
these books
until they gather
on my memories
pages

**sometimes
our eyes meet
across a crowded
conversation & this
is what i imagine
happens as stars
align & glow**

sometimes
i fall asleep
my comforter clinched
in on itself
& wrapped by my
arms & when i wake
each morning
i leave my bed
a mess of waves
i guess i imagine
i may one day find
you hiding among
the wrinkles

i never do, but tomorrow
is not today & my
tomorrows are full
of hopes

\*

sometimes
my plan A's
plummet
directly into
failure
& burn in
to ash & dust
so i wipe away
my eyes & work
my ways
through 25
other letters
as one of them
has to find
a path to
your heart

& if that fails
i guess i gotta
get a new plan
A

goto start

sometimes i let
my mouth fall empty
& let the poets pen
tongue my words
into a scream
because i know you
can decipher
the way my heart beats

## 60/40

sometimes
i want to press
my body in
to your body
& see if our
hearts play
the same music

& sometimes
i want to press
my body in to
yours
for other
reasons

sometimes
the moon lounges
about the stars
& the night
looks like a giant
smiley face

& i don't know
what the fuck
it finds so funny
coz i am here
& she is there
& even though
only one letter
separates here
from there, that
is more than millions
of miles for my arms
to reach across

so i guess he smiles
at my pain & arms
that only reach around
myself

\*

**sometimes
my arms beg
to weave
themselves into
your body & tangled
into your triceps
& everything
else to calm your
warring heart**

sometimes
the i love you's
are premature
like an orgasm
& your face
is flush & drips
with shame

& sometimes
you can't even
get it up

sometimes
our fingers braid
as the nights blanket
cascades over our eyes

＊

you may try
to push me
away as defenses
go on full alert
& that is okay
coz i may try
to dig my heels
in & leave
cleat marks
on your heart
i apologize
i'm not ready
to go

\*

sometimes
my body
heart
mind
all, seeks
the intimacy of
your mind & heart
our brains
sweaty & worn
out conversation
rather than from
our vulnerable bodies
press & pull
against each other

see... one lasts 45
or usually 5 minutes
& what want
lasts much longer

sometimes
it is the extended
goodnights
broken across
time & miles
& miles & more
miles & i pretend
it's my arms
draped over you
& not just blankets
taking up space
owed to my arms
& chest & legs
& heart

sometimes
only my eyes
select your body
while my heart
disagrees
seeking play
time within your heart
& mind

& usually wins

but my eyes still
get to play

sometimes she
she sleeps the morning
away & as my body
melts into work
& the blanket she's
wrapped in

scented of nicotine
& tar & i consider
picking up smoking so
all my things smell of her

huddled in bed
she presses her
ear into my chest
& my arms
are the jewelry
decorating her body

listen to my heart-
though, sometimes
it uses my mouth
to speak

sometimes your lips
taste of mint & nicotine
& when i'm nibbling
at your neck
i can taste the words
before they adorn
your mouth

they taste of black
licorice & sometimes
sarcasm & i like it

**all of the above**

sometimes
clarity tastes
of cherry
pies & i
don't want it
i hate cherry
pies & when i
look into your
eyes now - some
things hazy
& i ask if it is
me

or if there are
too many
inclusions
included
far too many

*

she chews words
in her sleep & every
time my bodies alarm
goes off; three am
four am & so on
i listen, trying to untwist
& decipher
what she is trying
to tell me
& every night i fail
i suppose
i always have
tomorrow night

\*

& sometimes i
wish i was
that man waltzing
clumsy through you (r)
dreams where questions
lead to satisfying
answers & not
my insincere & silly
sneers.

❋

**i don't know what
my tomorrow holds
though i want all
my tomorrows to hold
you**

sometimes love
just does not
fit &

i check my balcony
to see if she's there still
cigarette to her lips
cancer making love
to her lungs

i still smell you
on my blanket.
Find long red hairs
in my sink or
tangling me

i guess i should
wash my face more
but i won't
& i won't clean
my blanket until
long after the scent
escapes my memories

sometimes love
doesn't fit & we
argue with silence
or eyes too heavy
with temporary annoyance

& it doesn't fit
now, but i don't care

because you do fit
snugly into my chest
when we hug or when
we watch infomercials
or your lips taste
of tomorrow & fire
& i'd normally hate
that taste but...
you fit too snug among
my thoughts

or because you baby
talk under your breath
& whisper secrets in your
sleep or roll closer
than solo sleepers prefer

but sometimes, it just
doesn't fit... i guess

sometimes
you want to wear
3 extra pairs of socks
or tighten up that belt
so it does...

but i'm still a growing boy
& take my vitamins & this milk
tastes of maybe flavored tomorrows

**logic does not interest
me, if that means
moving on...**

sometimes
& weeks later
i still find you (r)
delinquent hairs
wrapped in my me
which is fine
though i wonder
do you sneak
into my bed & dig
your ear into my chest
as i dream & then
hide as my alarms
shriek

& i wonder
how many different
stars i should bribe
with wishes before
you decide to stay
through the nights
again

## Bio

Damon taught your favorite rapper how to rap.

He was almost a member of the Beatles, but he was too handsome and had no musical talent.

He's had poetry published in various small magazines. But none of that matters now as this self published chapbook is the pinnacle of his success as a writer.

Sometimes, he is an MFA student.

www.ingramcontent.com/pod-product-compliance
Lightning Source LLC
Chambersburg PA
CBHW061347040426
42444CB00011B/3133